JAMES TRONE

The Holland Method

Path + Practice

Dawnos™

First published by Dawnos Publishing 2026

First edition

ISBN: 979-8-218-81880-7

This book was professionally typeset on Reedsy.
Find out more at reedsy.com

To Mark Holland Trone – you are always loved, you made a difference, and you will always be remembered.

Contents

Foreword

Rule one: Never meet your heroes.

I broke that rule when I walked into a complete stranger's therapy office, barely hanging on—spiritually, emotionally, and physically limping through life. My relationship with James steered me out of my dark night of the soul. And it didn't happen the way I thought it would.

At first, I met James, the healer, the therapist. I came into his office in the middle of chronic piles of shit: panic attacks, depression, family deaths, divorce, the whole storm. When he asked me to close my eyes and "dive in," as he calls meditation that day, I was genuinely terrified. I didn't want to see what was underneath because I was sure I'd find hell. Cause hell was what I felt like. I didn't feel safe in my own body.

The truth is, that day I was hoping for a quick fix. As an athlete and performer, I wanted the playbook—the step-by-step program that would heal me. I wasn't looking to "dive in". But that moment ended up being the beginning of my journey back to myself... back to home.

What I found wasn't a formula. It was a sacred space. A space that allowed every side of me to come up—even the sides I hated—to be loved. A space where every emotion could come up without judgment. A space that showed me I didn't have to "thrive" my way into coming "home". But I was already there.

That's what The Holland Method is. That's who James is. If you're looking for a quick fix or a neat step-by-step plan, this isn't that. But what you'll find here is better: like a kind advice from a father, tough gut-punch honesty like a brother, and wisdom from someone who's bled for it in his own life.

Rule two: Never let your therapist become a friend.

Technically, this is still true cause James is more like a best friend or a big brother than just a "friend". Ever since I was a boy, I couldn't become a true fan of anything until I knew that artist or actor or athlete was a good person or meant what he said: authentic. James Trone is full blooded — who he is — and more, and this book and meditations are just the start. I'm a testimony still being written by his work as a client and now a proud friend.

This book isn't a 10-step program — it's an invitation to "dive in". I came into James' office looking to be fixed — what I learned was that I already was. What I wanted was control—what I found was freedom in the uncontrollable, a beautiful surrender into the unknown. I was looking for a quick fix — what I found was a way of life. And that's what I hope you find as you turn the page.

— Judah Akers of Judah & The Lion

Preface

HOW TO USE THIS BOOK

The Holland Method is not meant to be read once and set aside. It's an unfolding plan to be practiced — a rhythm that deepens over time.

At **www.hollandmethod.co**, you'll find access to the companion workbook, meditations, videos, and digital worksheets that align with each chapter. These tools are designed to help translate the ideas in these pages into daily life — to move the work from understanding into lived experience.

At minimum, begin with **The Work (A Daily Check-In)** — the core and backbone of this book. It's a simple daily rhythm — a kind of inner workout plan. You can find it in the *Free Downloads* section of the website.

There is no single way to move through this journey. Some begin with the meditations, others with journaling or the reflective questions at the end of each section. All that is asked is that you engage with yourself and return often to your own inner space. This book is an invitation: to the quiet work of remembering who you are beneath all the noise. Let's go!

Introduction

"Our deepest fear is not that we are inadequate. Our deepest fear is that we are powerful beyond measure. It is our light, not our darkness that most frightens us." - Marianne Williamson

The Holland Method was born out of my journey, shaped by both choice and circumstance, by seasons when I actively sought healing and by others when pain, confusion, or loss gave me no option but to go inward. A personal tragedy marked the beginning of a series of life pivots that ultimately pointed me home. In March of 2000, I lost my youngest brother, Mark (Holland), to suicide. That single moment created a definitive before and after in my life. His death reshaped my family, my choices, and my very sense of self. Even now, I catch myself navigating decisions made from that wounded place.

I named The Holland Method after him because his life, and his absence, have remained a constant presence in mine. A portrait of him hangs in my office: a quiet, steady reminder of why I do this work. Because it's not just about healing old wounds—it's about transformation. It's about taking pain and shaping it into something meaningful, something that offers hope.

We often talk about healing as a concept, but real transformation happens when we show up for the work. I use that phrase intentionally. The Work is the daily, deliberate practice of meeting ourselves—our pain, our patterns, our potential—with courage and compassion. It's not a quick fix, but a steady rhythm of returning to truth. Over the past two decades, I've explored countless therapeutic approaches both personally and with clients. Slowly, through study, practice, and reflection, I began to shape what I found most useful into a single, structured path. The Holland Method is the result of that work.

Before becoming a therapist, I built a successful career in commercial real estate. At one point, I was named Vice President at one of the country's largest firms, and I had just helped lead the leasing of The Pinnacle at Symphony Place, one of Nashville's most prestigious office buildings. But as that building rose into the skyline, I felt increasingly empty. Despite its external success, it began to feel like an empty shell, impressive from the outside, but hollow on the inside. Around that time, I began doing my inner work and entered therapy for the first time, joining a men's group where we practiced real authenticity and vulnerability. Something in me woke up. A deeper part of myself, long dormant, began to rise. I realized I wanted to feel alive again. I wanted to help others reconnect with their hearts, too. That awakening led me to leave one career path and begin another. Over time, I began gathering the practices that would become The Holland Method.

A mentor of mine once told me, "Following the voice of the inner child, the dreamer, can be deeply disruptive. It often feels risky, even reckless." But I've learned that when we follow that voice with wisdom, in community, and from a place of deep knowing, it won't lead us astray. That became a guiding truth for me: Sometimes the soul asks us to live boldly—to become more fully alive. Because when we ignore that voice, we begin to suppress our passion. And when we suppress our passion, we often become depressed or act out in harmful ways.

At its heart, The Holland Method offers both a path and a practice. Because while we can't always control what happens in life, we can choose how we engage with it. That's the heart of this work: bringing love to life. But to do that, we must first turn inward. We must honor the places we've been hurt, the parts of ourselves we've abandoned, and allow awareness to lead us into a new way of being. Many people arrive at this kind of work overwhelmed, as if they're wandering through a vast inner landscape without a map. Then questions arise: *What do I even want? Where am I going? What's being asked of me? What does it mean to connect with my soul, or listen to my deeper self?*

The Holland Method is meant to be that map—a framework to create a meaningful daily rhythm. I'm convinced that if we don't begin the day by reconnecting with the truth, if we don't set an intention for how we want to move through life, we'll fall back into the same loops and patterns. This method is shaped by over 15 years of practice, integrating the somatic (body), cognitive (thoughts), emotional (feelings), and subconscious (deeper psyche) layers of our being. But this is more than a philosophy. It's a lived, tangible practice. The beauty of The Holland Method lies in how it helps you navigate through the full spectrum of yourself. By offering practices to move through old patterns, emotional blocks, and limiting beliefs, while guiding you back to the truth of who you are.

I see this through the lens of two ways of being: the Ego Body and the Whole Body. The Ego Body holds the weight of our past; old energy, limiting beliefs, protective patterns, and emotional residue we've carried for years, often unconsciously. The Whole Body, in contrast, is marked by openness, grounded presence, and a felt sense of peace. It is not about perfection, but integration. And the movement from the Ego Body into the Whole Body is not always smooth. It can feel deeply uncomfortable: stirring resistance, old stories, and reactive emotions. This discomfort isn't a sign that something's wrong. It's a signal that you're stepping into a deeper level of awareness.

This is where *The Holland Method* comes in. It offers the tools: daily practices, reflections, movement, breath work, emotional processing, and intention-setting, to help guide that shift. These tools help you stay present, metabolize discomfort, and slowly return to the wholeness that has always been within you. The Holland Method provides real-time practices to help dissolve and shift these energies (physically, emotionally, and mentally) so that we can return to our true essence: love and wholeness. At the heart of this work is learning to recognize the two voices within us: the voice of love and the voice of fear. The goal is to develop the ability to trust, listen, and move in alignment with love rather than fear. This model is here to guide you through that process.

Finally, The Holland Method is organized around nine distinct states of transformation. These states aren't linear. They are cyclical and alive. They were inspired by the work of Richard Rohr[1] and Ken Wilber[2], particularly Rohr's articulation of the spiritual growth journey. Over the last decade, I've adapted that arc into a model that reflects my own experience and the work I've done with clients.

Here's how the book is organized:

Chapters 1–3: Foundations

- **The Work:** A Daily Rhythm
- **The Problem:** A Virtual Reality
- **The Solution:** A Move Inward

Chapters 4–12: The Nine States of Inward Transformation

1. **Body**
2. **Thoughts**
3. **Emotions**
4. **Smaller Self**
5. **Grief**
6. **Powerless**
7. **Larger Self**
8. **Connection**
9. **Wholeness**

You can access all meditations, videos, and worksheets for each chapter at www.hollandmethod.co. The worksheet below will be explored more deeply in the next chapter.

THE WORK

A DAILY RHYTHM AND PRACTICE

✓	**VISION** (Morning)	ALIGNING YOUR LIFE WITH WHAT TRULY MATTERS TO YOUR SOUL.
	JOURNALING	LISTENING TO YOUR INNER WORLD AND GIVING IT A VOICE.
	AFFIRMATION	REORIENTING YOUR MIND TOWARD LOVE, WORTH, AND POSSIBILITY.
	MEDITATION	RETURNING TO PRESENCE BY QUIETING THE MIND AND LISTENING WITHIN.
	READING	REORIENTATING TO TRUTH, OFFERING INSPIRATION AND ALIGNMENT WITH WHO YOU ARE AND WHERE YOU'RE GOING
	PAUSING	STEPPING OUT OF AUTOPILOT TO RECONNECT WITH YOUR PURPOSE.
	RESISTANCE	FACING THE PLACES WE AVOID - AND MOVING THROUGH IT UNLOCKING ENERGY AND CLARITY.
	PHYSICAL MOVEMENT	SHIFTING YOUR PHYSICAL STATE, TO RESTORE YOUR EMOTIONAL BALANCE.
	VISION (Evening)	REVIEWING THE DAY - SPACE FOR REFLECTION AND ALIGNMENT BEFORE REST.

1

The Work: A Daily Rhythm

"All of humanity's problems stem from man's inability to sit quietly in a room alone." —Blaise Pascal

For more than a decade working with clients in therapeutic settings, one truth has stood out above everything else: we all have to do the work. I often tell my clients: you're spending good money, sitting with me for an hour, maybe an hour and a half, each week or every other week, and that's valuable. The conversations matter. But if you really want to experience lasting change, if you want to feel something shift inside, then it requires doing the work every day, and I have found it most helpful in the quiet of the morning.

"Doing the Work"

The phrase "doing the work" originated with a close friend of mine, known as Hap or Happy. He was a former Navy SEAL and a member of SEAL Team Six (DEVGRU). I got to know him through my brother, and for several years we'd head to Colorado together on long elk-hunting trips, backpacking deep into the Rockies. On my first trip with him, he knew I was a therapist, and naturally, I was curious about his background. He had completed ten combat tours, an experience that left its mark. As we spent more time together, our conversations naturally drifted into trauma, healing, and mental health.

Many in special forces find that a different kind of battle begins after combat, when the intensity of special operations gives way to the quiet pace of civilian life. The transition can be disorienting, and support is often limited. Hap decided to pursue healing for himself. As we discussed mental health in greater depth, he put it in simple yet powerful terms. He said, "It's all about doing the work. You've got to do the work." For him, "the work" wasn't vague or abstract. It included physical exercise and nutrition, cognitive and emotional therapy, deep inner dives, somatic practices, and meditation. It was a full-spectrum commitment to healing: body, mind, and soul.

That phrase stuck with me: "doing the work". It wasn't just something he said once; it came up again and again. It left a lasting impression on me. Since then, it has carried over into my personal life and my work with clients. It became a mantra, a framework, and a truth I've returned to often: healing takes work. Real, intentional work. But it's holy work. It's a bit like hiring a fitness trainer. You meet once a week, but if you don't do the workouts on your own in between sessions, you won't see results.

This inner work is no different. That's why I welcome this work. This program, this daily rhythm, is designed to give you the structure and space to begin that work on your own. To explore the deeper layers of yourself. To begin discovering aspects of yourself that you may not even have realized existed. And let me be clear: this work does not approach you as something to be fixed. It does not treat you as a problem or a pathology. This is about entering a much larger discovery, a journey of uncovering your true self, the wholeness that's always been within you

The Work – A Daily Rhythm for Engaging Your Life

Imagine receiving a book with all the answers; solutions to every problem, clear directions on how to live your life. Sounds ideal, right? But here's the catch - even if we had all the answers, we'd still have to live the life. We'd still have to face ourselves. Knowing the path doesn't spare us from walking it through challenges, emotions, and the rawness of lived experience.

That's why Blaise Pascal's quote resonates so deeply - the idea that so much of our trouble stems from the inability to sit quietly in a room alone. Even with all the answers, we still have to sit with ourselves, and that is often where our suffering lies. And that's where practice comes in. It's not about escaping discomfort, but about learning to engage with it. To meet the shadow aspects of who we are with honesty, so we can grow into something deeper, a larger and expanded life.

In this first chapter, we begin with something simple but foundational: a daily rhythm. This rhythm grounds you in a steady way of navigating your life, creating a sense of continuity, presence, and support amid daily demands.

We all need some structure. Without it, we drift. But too much structure, too rigid a plan—and we start to lose touch with the heart of why we're doing it. That's the delicate balance this rhythm aims to hold: not coasting through your days on autopilot, and not forcing yourself through another self-improvement checklist. Establishing this rhythm is a daily practice of coming back to yourself, again and again.

This rhythm includes a handful of simple practices:

- Creating *The Vision*
- Journaling
- Affirmations
- Meditation (10-minutes)
- Reading
- Pausing throughout the day to step out of autopilot
- Physical movement—running, walking, stretching, yoga, weights
- Resistance - One "Avoided" Task (bills, taxes, emails, etc.)
- A nightly review of *The Vision*

These practices are intentionally small and doable, but don't mistake them for insignificant. Together, they create a significant container for transformation. You meditate, so you don't have to start meditating in the middle of a crisis. You pause throughout the day to avoid getting trapped in reactivity. These are preparatory practices that support how you meet and live your life. It is about presence. Let it be less about discipline and more about devotion. These practices help you live more intentionally and respond differently to life.

This daily rhythm unwinds old patterns and builds a new internal architecture that can support the deeper work we'll explore in the rest of this method. It tunes your inner antenna to a deeper frequency. You begin to hear the deeper *you* that's always been there, but that needs space to rise, to speak, and to guide. You don't need to force it. You don't need to do it perfectly. You just need to begin. And over time, you may discover a rhythm that brings you back to what has always been within you.

Creating *The Vision*

To start, we all need a vision. Without one, we don't know where we're going or what we are doing. But before we can name a vision, we must first set clear, honest intentions for the life we want to create and fully realize. This process of envisioning begins with a few essential steps and questions that bring focus:

1. Clarify Your Call

- What do I truly want?
- Where am I being called?
- What does my deepest self ask of me?[3]

2. Identify Your Gifts

- What are my strengths?
- Where am I uniquely gifted?
- What can I offer the world that only I can bring?

3. Establish a Structure

- How must I shape my life to support this vision?
- What changes are necessary to make it work?
- What daily commitments will bring it into being?

4. Face the Obstacles

- What am I resisting?
- What's getting in my way?

5. Commit to Action - completing the daily tasks to get you there.

This is about living your vision and growing into who you were always meant to be. When you align with your calling, the energy to fulfill it will meet you. Create a vision not only for your life's work, but also for how you want to show up for your family, friends, and community.

Journaling

Journaling is often overlooked, or at least underestimated, as a transformational practice. We sometimes resist it, thinking we're only writing down what we already know. But the truth is, journaling can give voice to what is deep inside of us that needs to be voiced. It gives voice to our shadow and true essence, which we will discuss in more detail. It helps us bring forth what we have been suppressing. By simply sitting down, you can access these tools, allowing you to write without editing. You begin to access the more hidden parts of your inner world: the feelings, thoughts, and beliefs that live just beneath the surface of awareness. The more you write, especially in a free-flow state, the more you begin to uncover the deeper layers of emotion, memory, and meaning that may have gone unspoken for years.

There are two powerful techniques I recommend to begin this process:

> 1 - <u>Stream-of-Consciousness Journaling</u> - This is simple and raw. You write whatever comes: feelings, thoughts, memories, questions, without stopping, censoring, or correcting. You might start by asking: What am I feeling right now? What is this part of me trying to tell me? Let the words lead you. Let it be messy and real.
>
> 2 - <u>Non-Dominant Hand (Inner Child) Journaling</u> - This technique is especially effective when addressing vulnerability, unmet needs, or past wounds. Try writing with your non-dominant hand, as if you are letting your inner child speak. Because you're not used to writing with this hand, it naturally puts you in a more tender, unguarded state, and what emerges often comes straight from the heart. Then, with your dominant hand, respond from your adult self, offering care, presence, and compassion. This back-and-forth dialogue helps bridge the distance between the self

that once felt lost or unseen and the self that now knows how to listen. Journaling is a quiet doorway inward, a daily practice of presence and a return to your own voice.

Affirmations

Affirmations can sometimes feel like empty exercises in "positive thinking"—as if you're trying to trick yourself into a better mindset. Yet affirmations are far more powerful: they help set your state of mind, influencing not just your thoughts but also how you live and interact in the world. They reveal whether you're operating from a state of empowerment or stuck in what I call the vortex of negativity. Think of affirmations as anchors or light posts along the way:

Morning Anchor: The very first thing you do upon waking—recite a positive affirmation.

Evening Anchor: The last thought before you sleep—offer yourself another uplifting affirmation.

By bookending your day with these two anchors, you create a framework for staying anchored in truth. The real healing happens when you carry those affirmations with you throughout the day, reminding yourself, for instance:

- "I am love."
- "I am enough."
- "I can succeed."
- "I am OK as I am."

These simple phrases keep you from slipping back into a trance of separation and negativity. Every time you return to an affirmation, you actively reorient yourself to loving regard and openness, creating the space to truly absorb its benefits.

Meditation

Meditation is an incredibly effective practice because it cultivates presence through breathwork, stillness, and deep listening. Often, your conscious (egoic) mind has no idea whether it's "working," and that's exactly the point: it's a subconscious invitation for something deeper in your system to arise.

Many dismiss meditation as "new age," but in reality, it's ancient; a practice of slowness and stillness. Meditation can take many forms, but at its core, it simply brings you back to the present moment: tuning into your body, anchoring in your breath, and quieting the mind so you're not swept up in the day's urgency.

A common misconception is that meditation means having a completely blank mind, free of all thoughts. That's not the goal. The true purpose of meditation is to observe your thoughts, emotions, and physical sensations—and then gently return to the present moment. It's entirely normal for your mind to wander; in fact, that's exactly why a regular practice is so valuable. Each time you notice a distraction and come back to your breath or body, you strengthen your capacity for focus and calm.

Throughout these chapters, you'll find guided meditations tailored to each topic. At the end of each chapter, under Meditative Practices, you'll see links to the specific meditations aligned with each chapter's theme. Whenever you're ready to deepen your practice, simply choose the recommended meditation for that chapter and let it guide you into greater presence and insight. All meditations are available under the artist name Dawnos on all the streaming services, so you can easily listen and integrate them into your daily rhythm wherever you are.

Reading

Reading, as part of the work, is both informational and transformational. It's not just about gaining knowledge, it's about reorienting yourself toward what you already know deep down. The right material doesn't simply teach; it reminds. Daily reading becomes a moment of integration, a way to align your conscious and unconscious mind with truth. It's a gentle reprogramming, a returning. Whether you're reading from The Holland Method, or the companion workbook, a daily reflection, or another source of wisdom, the goal is the same: to reconnect with what matters and to stay rooted in the direction you're moving. Inspiration from others can become fuel for your path. A few minutes each day reading something that speaks to your deeper self can create powerful shifts over time.

Pausing

Pausing is a simple yet powerful way to reorient yourself to the present moment and your reality whenever you begin to slip into old patterns or autopilot.

- Set an Alarm: Every few hours, set a gentle alert to remind you to pause.
- Take Three Minutes: Sit quietly and notice what's happening right now—what you're thinking, feeling, and doing.
- Reconnect: Return to your affirmation, your vision, and the intention for your day.
- Check In: Ask yourself, "How am I feeling? Am I in alignment with my purpose? Is there something I need to do differently?

Think of each pause like a pit stop throughout the day. It doesn't take much time, but it refreshes your focus, anchors you back to your purpose, and breaks the trance of separation and default modes of being. Over time, these micro-pauses become the foundation for greater presence, clarity, and ease in your daily life.

Physical Movement

Physical movement might seem obvious, but it's vital for two key reasons:

1 - Instant State Shift - Changing your body changes your mind. If you're stuck in negative thinking or emotions, stand up, step outside, or move your body to interrupt that cycle. This practical, tangible shift resets your state of being almost immediately.

2 - Long-Term Emotional Support - We are all familiar with the benefits of physical activity for our bodies. But what about the direct impact it can also have on

our emotional health? Moving your body releases endorphins, the brain's natural antidepressants, which are often more effective than any pill. Aim to eat foods to nourish your body. Stay hydrated. Because what you eat and drink also influences how you feel, pairing mindful movement with nutritious choices multiplies the benefit.

Each day, make it a point to get up and move. Even a brief walk or a few stretches can break the trance of negativity. Plan a regular workout you enjoy, whether that's yoga, running, weightlifting, pickleball, or another activity, and aim to step outside whenever you can. At the same time, aim to eat nourishing foods and stay hydrated. What you eat and drink directly affects your mood and energy. By combining mindful movement with healthy fuel, you'll tap into natural endorphins and create a reliable foundation for emotional well-being. No amount of reflection alone will shift your energy as reliably as physical movement. Commit to moving your body every day; your mind, mood, and overall well-being depend on it.

Resistance

Every day, we're faced with tasks we don't want to do. Some feel mundane. Others stir up fear. But underneath it all, resistance is usually rooted in old programming, stories we've carried for a long time. And these stories establish patterns of avoidance. This is where the work comes in. We can learn to predict where resistance shows up. We learn to practice staying engaged. The daily solution is to identify what needs to be done. Write it out and then do it. If you're avoiding a workout, move your body. If you're putting off paying bills, sit down and pay them. If you're resisting filing your taxes, file them. Because on the other side of resistance is aliveness.

Nightly Review of *The Vision*

Every night before you go to bed is an invitation to reflect. As you're preparing for sleep, return to the affirmation of the day. Meditate on it. Then review your vision. Think back on what you learned, what went well, and what didn't. Come back again to that affirmation. Let it anchor you. The point isn't to overanalyze; it's to gently set your subconscious in motion. Because even if we don't fully understand it, the subconscious keeps working while we sleep: processing, integrating, sorting. It's been said we're responsible for our dreams during sleep, because who else could be?

So by revisiting your vision and reaffirming your intention, you're helping shape that inner terrain. You're giving your unconscious something to hold through the night. And that's a powerful way to prepare not just for sleep, but for how you will engage the next day.

Meditative Practice (under the Artist name Dawnos on various music platforms)

- Dawnos *Oriented* Album // Track 1 - Vision & Purpose
- Dawnos *Oriented* Album // Track 2 - Ocean Breath
- Dawnos *Oriented* Album // Track 3 - Inner Temple

Action Steps

1. Will you commit to setting aside time this week to write out your vision? (Use the Meditation Track 1 as a guide.)
2. Can you try—even for just one day—the practice where you feel the most resistance?

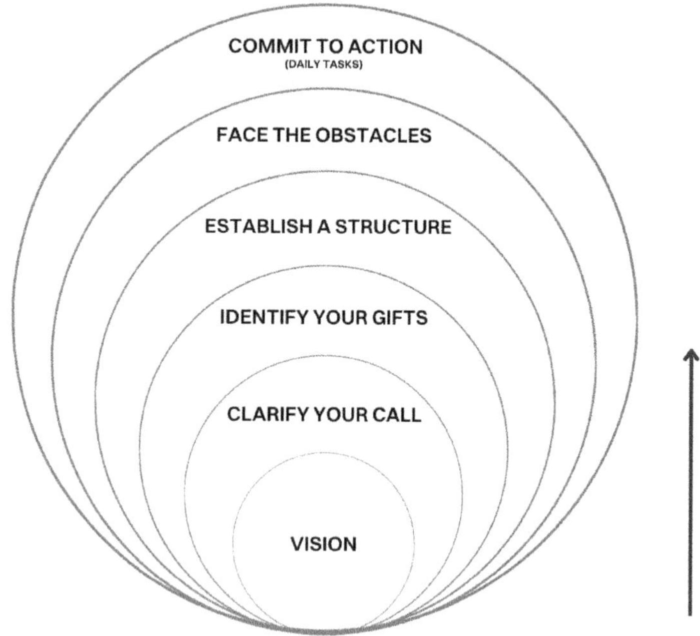

2

The Problem: A Virtual Reality

"Until you make the unconscious conscious, it will direct your life, and you will call it fate." — Carl Jung

The story comes from James Finley, shared on his podcast, Turning to the Mystics[4]. It goes like this:

> *One day, you're driving home, and off in the distance, you notice an incredible sunset. On a whim—something you don't usually do—you pull over, get out of your car, and simply stand there, taking it in. You give yourself to the sunset, and in a sense, the sunset gives itself to you. You're lost in the moment, lost in time. Minutes go by, and you don't even notice. Fifteen, thirty minutes pass before you realize you need to head home. You get back in your car and drive off, returning to daily life. When you get back into the car, you check your text messages and quickly get pulled back into the busyness of life— responsibilities, all the usual things. And before long, you've forgotten about the beauty of that sunset.*

But then there's a second story.

When you arrive home, you open the mail and find a letter from an estate attorney. You discover that a distant relative, recently deceased, has left you their entire estate in their will. Skeptical, you investigate. You meet with the attorney, verify the documents, and confirm that it's all true. You've inherited an extraordinary property. You drive out to the estate and walk the grounds, taking it all in. The house is everything you could have imagined—perfectly designed, exactly your style. You walk around, peering through the windows at the library, the great room, and the kitchen, and you're filled with excitement and gratitude. Later that weekend, you invite your friends and family out for a cookout by the pool house. Afterward, you show them around the grounds. But there's one problem: you don't have a key to get inside the house. So you walk around the exterior, looking in through the windows, admiring everything from the outside.

Next week, you meet with your psychotherapist. After listening to your story, the therapist looks at you and says, "I won't lie to you on this one—you're already inside the mansion. You've been in the mansion all along." You pause, confused. "How could that be?" you ask. And that's when the words of Jesus echo: 'Let those who have eyes, see; let those who have ears, hear.'"

The Problem: Living in a Limited Reality

The problem lies not only in our inability to see ourselves clearly but also in a deeply ingrained sense of separation. It's an old conditioning, an outdated program we've carried for years. You know you're living in this limited reality when someone offers you a compliment or expresses love, and while you *hear* it in your mind, you don't *feel* it in your body—this deep sense of love. There's a disconnect, and that's the problem.

You also experience this limited reality when you're moving through your day feeling stressed, down, or disconnected, when life feels heavy or dull. This is what it feels like to be living separately and small. And from this state, we develop survival strategies: perfectionism, procrastination, addictive patterns, or a diminished view of who we are. We start to believe things like *I am not enough* or *I can't*. These beliefs cast the shadows of our separate, smaller self.

We can think of these limitations through different models:

- The Trauma Model—the ways unprocessed pain shapes our perception
- The Patterns Model—the unconscious strategies we use to survive
- The Story Model—the narratives we repeat about who we are and what's possible

Each of these models keeps us locked in living small. They are different faces of the same shadow, ways we stay safe and stuck. And because of this, we limit ourselves, our hearts, and our dreams. This is the inner violence of living separately and small.

What's often overlooked is how this limited reality perpetuates an inner cycle of violence. The way we fix, force, shame, and guilt ourselves to "get better" only reinforces the belief that there's something wrong with us. It compounds the problem, keeping us caught in the pattern of living separately and small. This is subtle but real, an ongoing inner violence that keeps us closed off from the truth of who we are. The problem is that we have been chasing the wrong person. We have been chasing our Shadow or often running from it.

This shadow is made up of the parts of us we'd rather not see. It's the anger, the lust, and the rage. It is these shameful behaviors, the emotions we resist the most, the parts we try to run from. And yet, they're still there. The work isn't to eliminate the shadow but to become aware of it. To recognize that while it's part of us, it doesn't have to control us. The more we accept that these parts exist simply because we're human, the less we live in denial. The shadow will show up. That's inevitable. But the more we listen to what it's trying to tell us, the more we create a connection with it—rather than being overpowered by it.

But there is another way. By creating a space within yourself, healing begins. The key is not to fix or force. The key is to *nurture* ourselves back to Reality, the truth of who we are. Our Soul is always leading us toward expansion. And the way forward is gentle: slowing down, opening up, letting go, and trusting the process rather than controlling it

This isn't a "fixing" model; it's a return. And as we move toward expansion, resistance will inevitably arise. Resistance often masquerades as comfort: it's familiar, it feels safe. But stepping out of the comfort zone and into expansion is like crossing into a new frontier. It's unknown, and living separately and small cannot see past its current limits. It cannot fathom that we are far more than we think we are at this moment. The practice of noticing. This module is about starting to notice when we are separate and small. To catch ourselves in the moment and recognize, Oh, here it is again. And instead of buying into it, we create a little space, soften, and stay open. We choose not to believe everything the limited self tells us. This is where the return begins.

Meditative Practice

- Dawnos *Oriented* Album // Track 4 - Virtual Reality
- Dawnos *Oriented* Album // Track 5 - Clouds
- Dawnos *Oriented* Album // Track 6 - Sacred Space

Action Steps

1. What is one honest intention you can name for your life right now?
2. Which of your strengths or gifts do you most want to offer the world?
3. What pattern, story, or unresolved trauma might be holding you back from fully stepping into your vision?
4. What is one small change you could make this week to interrupt that pattern?

THE SHADOW

THREE LENSES THAT BLOCK SEEING CLEARLY

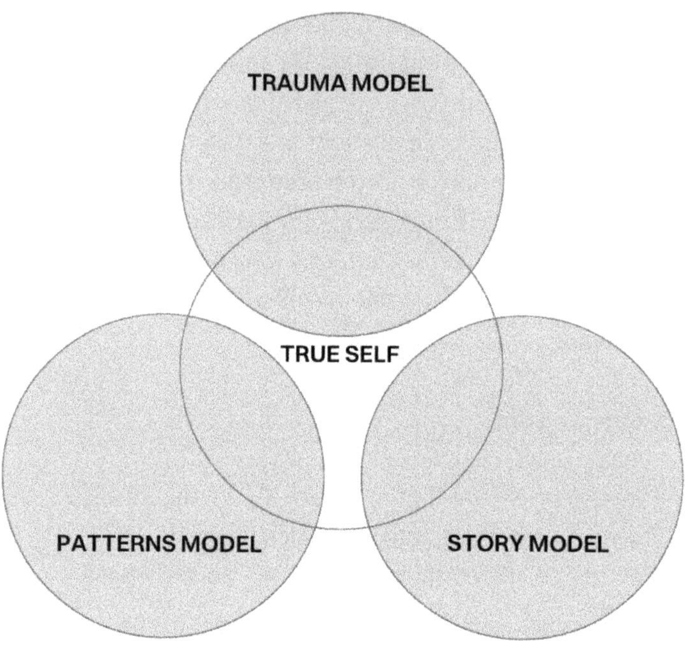

3

The Solution: A Move Inward

"We carry inside us the wonders we seek outside us."— Rumi

An excerpt from Rick Rubin's Tetragrammaton podcast[5] interview with Will Smith explores the theme of going inward.

> *Rick Rubin asks Will Smith, "Tell me about how do you view success? Like what do you see success as and has it changed from when you were young?"*
>
> *Will Smith - "It's definitely transformed. I wanted to be number one. I wanted to be the biggest actor on earth, manifest destiny. The biggest, the best in everything...And the thing that happened is I thought with that would come love and protection. I realized at least that you get to the top of all of that and you're still the same insecure little boy you were before you did all of that. Now you just don't have any distractions from it anymore."*

Rick Rubin - "Yes, and now the version I've seen and experienced is, you can get hopeless because I spent all of my time and effort to solve the problem. And I did it. And it didn't do anything. And now what do I do?"

Will Smith - "And it can make it worse."

Rick Rubin - "You can become hopeless because you're thinking, you have the solution and you go for the solution and you spend your whole life to achieve the solution and the solution is not the solution."

Will Smith - "And I got it exactly how I wanted it, beyond anything I could have possibly imagined, it was perfect and beyond. And still didn't solve the problem. You know, so there's an existential terror that kicks in when you realize that there's actually nothing in the world to solve that problem. So that is the introduction to the abyss."

Rick Rubin - "In some ways, you can't really get depressed until your dreams come true."

Will Smith - "Right. Like when your dreams come true, you realize, hmm, now what?" The two places that I think you can get depressed. One is rock bottom. When you hit rock bottom and literally you're in like the worst circumstance you could have ever possibly imagined. And you know, you hear that in AA they talk about rock bottom is when your life begins. And there's a corresponding place that I call cliff top. There's nowhere to go. It's the both ends of existence where there's nowhere to go, but inward. And it's hard to explain. And you can't even truly have a conversation if someone hasn't experienced one or the other."

Rick Rubin - "It's completely unrelatable to everybody unless you have the experience."

The Solution – Moving Inward

That sense of having nowhere else to turn, whether at your lowest low or your highest high, points us toward the same truth: the real frontier is inside. With all outward options exhausted, the only path forward is inward. This module marks a turning point in our journey. After seasons marked by pain, discontent, or exhaustion from external fixes, we're invited to direct our attention away from the old habit of striving outward toward a new center: our own inner landscape. The solution isn't found in more effort or control, but in connection: connecting with ourselves, with presence, and with the deeper source that guides meaningful change.

Before we can hear what's true, we learn to step back from what's loud. Many traditions speak of the observer, the witness, awareness itself. "Awareness looking back at awareness" can sound abstract, but it simply means stepping back from our roles and stories and resting as the one who notices them. From that soulful center, we remember we're more than our masks. This is the both/and: the love we call God seems beyond us, yet it lives within us. We're invited to co-create with it, not as a concept, but as a felt reality. So the question isn't only "Who am I?" but "Who is the one seeing, thinking, and feeling right now—the one aware of all this?" Said plainly, this is your inner loving parent re-parenting your inner child (we'll practice this in Chapter 7).

We begin to connect with Source, a presence that is both within us and all around us. Source lives in all things. It exists everywhere, yet also moves through us like scattered fragments waiting to be remembered and reassembled. It's our soul, our higher self, and our truest knowing. And it's always been there, quietly waiting beneath the noise of our conditioning. To access Source, we must slow down. We open up and allow ourselves to receive. This is not a performance or a technique. It's a return by softening and a willingness to see with new eyes and listen with keener ears. When we do, we begin to see and hear life more clearly; no longer filtered through the lens of fear, past wounds, or egoic striving.

Three essential elements of Source help guide this return:

- **Vision (Light)** – an internal illumination, a kind of intuitive clarity and joy that rises from within. It's not about "feeling good," but about being aligned. It shows us the way forward, one small moment at a time.
- **Voice (Sound)** – the original language of the soul. The still, small voice within. It's gentle, timeless, and resonant. It calls us inward and reminds us of our innocence, our wholeness.
- **Love** – the boundless current we're meant to receive and channel. We don't manufacture it; connected to Source, we become its vessel. The work is not just about knowing this, but about feeling it and living it.

When we are truly present, we create space for these qualities to emerge. Presence disrupts the loops of our old stories. It creates flow and clarity. It restores access to the deeper self that has never been lost, only forgotten. To help anchor this experience, we introduce the *SOURCE* acronym, a meditative and practical tool for connecting to the deeper current within you:

- **S** – Seek
- **O** – Open
- **U** – Unknown
- **R** – Resource
- **C** – Compassion
- **E** – Experience

Each word is a portal, a posture of the heart. This practice is not about arriving somewhere, but about inhabiting your life from a more grounded, loving place. And from here, from this connection, you begin to hear what your soul is asking of you. You begin to connect to this deeper sense of being. Not one driven by pressure or performance, but one shaped by resonance and truth. The energy to fulfill that original vision begins in this inward space. This is the beginning of a new way and yet an ancient way of being, one led not by fear or ego, but by the deeper truth of who you already are. What follows are simple tools to help you return to this center, especially when you feel it least.

Meditative Practice

- Dawnos *Oriented* Album // Track 7 - SOURCE
- Dawnos *Oriented* Album // Track 8 - Sourcing
- Dawnos *Oriented* Album // Track 9 - Healing Light

Action Steps

1. What is one way you can make more space to listen inward this week?
2. When do you feel most connected to God, Source, Love (whatever name you choose)?
3. What old narrative or belief makes it hard to trust this inward path?
4. When your mind or old habits try to pull you away, how will you gently return?

SOURCE

A TOOL TO AID IN ACCESSING A POWER GREATER THAN YOURSELF

S	SEEK	Invite a Higher Power, whether you call it God or define it as your Source, to be present with you in this moment.
O	OPEN	Stay open to hearing, observing, and listening for that Source. Be mindful of anything that may be hindering your connection.
U	UNKNOWN	Embrace the unknown found in silence and observation, allowing yourself to acknowledge any distractions that draw you away from this space.
R	RESOURCE	Invite the presence of those who have influenced your life—mentors, teachers, family, spiritual influences, even those no longer with us. If wisdom is needed, allow it in.
C	COMPASSION	Embrace receiving compassion and support from those who have come to mind.
E	EXPERIENCE	Embrace this moment fully; take note of the qualities, thoughts, and emotions that arise within you right now.

4

Body

"Your body is your subconscious mind." — Candace Pert

There was a man who lived most of his life a few inches above himself. He didn't know it, of course, not until much later. But looking back, he could see it clearly. He had been floating, always slightly removed from the life he was living. He was a father, a provider, a man who checked the boxes and lived a productive life. But often, when laughter happened around him, it felt like it was happening in another room. When pain came, he managed it, explained it, filed it away. He lived from the neck up, mastering logic, success, and productivity, but never quite learning how to *feel and be loved.*

Then one evening, after a quiet dinner, his teenage daughter said something so small, so ordinary, it could have drifted by like any other moment. "Dad, I felt kind of invisible with you at the party last night." That was all; there were no accusations or anger. Just a truth softly spoken. But something in him cracked. It wasn't the words themselves. It was what they *touched,* somewhere deep inside his chest, a place he hadn't visited in years. He tried to respond, tried to explain, but the more he spoke, the more distant he felt. Her eyes were kind, but they mirrored something he hadn't expected: sadness. That night, he couldn't sleep. His mind spun stories, ones filled with failure, regret, and shame. But unlike other nights, when he might've poured a drink or buried himself in a screen, this time he did something different. He sat still.

And for the first time, he listened; not to his thoughts, but to the *ache* beneath them. He noticed the tension in his gut. The tightening in his jaw. The weight in his chest. It was as if his body had been trying to speak for years, and he'd only just remembered how to listen. He placed a hand on his heart, another on his stomach, and sat with himself. And something began to soften. The negative thought loop slowed, and the shame began to dissolve. And beneath all the noise, there was a strange sense of... peace.

Over the weeks that followed, he began a quiet practice, not of perfection, but of presence. He walked more slowly and began breathing more deeply. He asked his body questions instead of issuing commands. And in doing so, something remarkable happened. He began to feel connected, not all the time, and not in dramatic ways. But in the small, sacred rhythms of his day, his daughter's laughter, the scent of morning coffee, the warm sun on his forearms. Life no longer passed him by. It met him.

One afternoon, while clearing brush at the edge of his backyard, he uncovered something unexpected: a small, rusted iron gate, half-swallowed by ivy and time. He didn't remember it. Or maybe he had simply forgotten. Behind it was an overgrown garden, wild and waiting. He stepped through the gate and stood in stillness.

Reconnecting to the Body

We return to the body, not as something to manage or fix, but as a sacred home for the soul. We shift from viewing the body as a burden or battleground to understanding it as an instrument of presence, healing, and purpose. Throughout our lives, the body is our constant companion. It carries not only our breath and movement but also our story; our memories, emotions, and unprocessed experiences. And yet, many of us spend years disconnected from it. We over-identify with the ego body, which operates in reaction, suppression, dissociation, and shame. Or, we leave the body entirely, numbing or bypassing its messages to avoid discomfort.

This disconnection creates suffering. But the body itself is not the source of pain; disconnection is. And connection is the way through. To reconnect with the body is to return to a deeper truth. It is to listen, to soften, and to feel what's been waiting to move. Within the body, unconscious energy takes shape as anxiety, grief, shame, or anger. This energy often spirals into what we call the vortex, a spinning field of emotion that keeps us locked in ego-body patterns. But this vortex can be interrupted. It can be softened. The task is to drop beneath it, not escape it, but move through it with awareness and compassion.

We introduce the Felt Sense Practice as a gateway to this process. It is a method of tuning in: of pausing, locating sensation, observing without judgment, and gently reuniting mind and body. When practiced regularly, it becomes a bridge that carries us out of reactivity and into presence. This work is not immediate. As with any detox, there may be a delay, a moment where old energy stirs before it shifts. But the body is wise. The energy you feel is not something to fear; it's something to meet with love. The paradox is that the more you engage with the body, the more it communicates. The more you listen, the more it heals.

There is a deeper invitation here: to know that you are *in* your body, but you are *more than* your body. And yet, this body is your vessel. This is where alchemy happens. This is where spirit takes form. When you reconnect to the body, you begin to reconnect with Source. And through that connection, the energy of transformation begins to move. This is the slow, sacred work of embodiment. It's not just about feeling better. It's about becoming whole.

Practice: Returning to the Body Through a Felt Sense

This simple four-step process helps you reconnect with the body, bringing awareness, presence, and softness to places that feel tight, stuck, or disconnected. It may seem simple enough to pass right over, but something powerful happens when we actually place our hands back on our body, particularly on the heart and the gut. In doing so, we bring attention back to ourselves in a direct, physical way. It is a remarkably straightforward, simple, and effective practice. Here is one way to work with it:

1. *Notice the Body* - Bring your attention to the body. What sensations are present? Is there contraction, tightness, numbness, or restlessness? These are often signatures of the Ego Body—a body holding onto unprocessed energy.
2. *Observe the Body* - Now become the observer. Notice where this energy is located—has it taken up residence in your chest, throat, stomach, or elsewhere? Notice how the mind may try to pull you into a narrative. Gently return your focus to the felt sense—the raw experience in the body. Try not to judge or analyze. Just be with what is.
3. *Hands on Heart + Gut* - Place one hand on your heart, the other on your belly. This is a simple gesture, but it serves as a powerful bridge, reconnecting mind and body. Feel the warmth of your hands. Feel the breath moving beneath them. Let this be a shift into the Whole Body—the part of you that is present, alive, and capable of holding what you feel with love.
4. *Felt Sense of Now* - Finally, settle into *this* moment. Allow the body to be as it is. If your awareness drifts to the past or future, gently return to the felt sense of now—the breath, the contact with the ground, the beating of your heart. Let the body be your anchor.

As you begin to notice and observe your body, it's helpful to engage with it in a way that moves you out of the egoic mind and into a deeper, more embodied awareness. These gentle inquiries are designed to slow down reactive thinking and open space for connection, insight, and integration. Use these prompts to enter the body's language, where stored emotions, memories, and energy often speak through sensation, color, shape, temperature, weight, and age.

These prompts help bypass the overthinking mind and allow your awareness to settle into your body; into a felt sense that offers clarity, compassion, and deeper healing.

Meditative Practice

- Dawnos *Oriented* Album // Track 10 - Felt Sense
- Dawnos *Oriented* Album // Track 11 - Grounding
- Dawnos *Oriented* Album // Track 12 - Energy Grid

Action Steps

1. When you pause right now, what sensations do you notice in your body?
2. Where do you feel tension or discomfort?
3. What story, past event, or identity might be tied to this sensation?
4. What is one movement or grounding practice you will try today?

FELT SENSE

A PRACTICE TO CONNECT TO THE BODY MORE DEEPLY

1	LOCATION	If the energy were located in the body, where would it be? Notice where your body is uncomfortable. Typically, it is the first place that comes to mind.
2	COLOR	Colors can represent energy. Connecting to colors it allows you to connect more to the energy. This is also part of Chakra work, which has been around for thousands of years and is represented by colors.
3	SHAPE | SYMBOL	Identifying a shape/symbol accesses a different part of the brain region.
4	WEIGHT	There is often a weight and heaviness to our ego body's pain. How heavy does it feel?
5	TEMPERATURE	Energy has a temperature to it. We will often feel hot, warm, or cold. Often it is related to different emotions. For example, anger is often heat whereas fear, shame, or loneliness is cold.
6	AGE	This question helps make a connection to older energy of the past most often of childhood that has been stored.

5

Thoughts

"We suffer more often in imagination than in reality." — Seneca

I want to share a common story, not a specific one, but an experience most of us have. It goes something like this:

You're meeting with someone; maybe an old friend, a client, or a family member. The conversation flows. You're relaxed, fully present, not guarding every word. Because you feel at ease, you speak freely. Maybe you even get a little animated or emotionally charged—not in a negative way toward them, but just fully being yourself in the moment, unfiltered and unedited.

Then, after you leave, something happens. You start replaying the conversation in your head. And as you replay it, you filter it through old narratives, old beliefs. Maybe the belief that "I'm too much," or "I shouldn't have said that," or "I'm in trouble now." You wonder what they must be thinking: "Did I offend them? Do they think less of me?" And suddenly, you've built an entire narrative in your mind, an entire story, based not on what actually happened, but on your own perception of how you think the conversation was received.

Here's the kicker, and this has happened to me many times. Later, when I reconnect with that friend or family member, I realize that the version I created in my head never existed. Sometimes I'll even bring it up: "Hey, I hope what I said didn't come across the wrong way." And more often than not, they'll look at me, confused, and say something like, "I don't even remember you saying that," or, "I wasn't offended at all." The whole situation I'd worked up in my mind didn't exist. I had created it entirely on my own.

The Practice: Exploring Your Thoughts

This module invites you into the inner landscape of your mind to begin to see, notice, and hear these thoughts with curiosity and compassion. At the heart of this work is one simple, transformative question: "Is this voice coming from love, or fear?"

Every day, your mind is filled with voices, narratives, and beliefs; some rooted in truth, others shaped by fear, past pain, or old conditioning. It can feel like a full-time training and work. The problem is that many negative thoughts go unnoticed, running in the background and quietly shaping how you feel and how you live. This module is about bringing those thoughts into the light—not to judge them, but to see them. You'll begin to recognize two distinct inner voices:

The voice of fear is loud, logical, anxious, and controlling. It often disguises itself as "reasonable" but keeps you spinning in projections, self-doubt, and separation. It pulls you into the past or the future, feeding stories of not-enoughness, abandonment, failure, or lack. The voice of Love, by contrast, is quieter. It's intuitive, kind, accepting, and rooted in the present. It speaks calmly. It holds space without judgment. It helps you see yourself and others through a lens of compassion and clarity. It often waits in stillness until you are ready to hear it.

This module is about learning to discern between these voices and, again and again, to choose the voice of love. You're not trying to get rid of fear, but you are learning how not to follow it. You're learning to hear your thoughts without letting them define you. This is the practice of returning to reality, one moment and thought at a time.

When a situation arises that doesn't feel peaceful or neutral, it's an invitation to pause and explore how you're seeing it. Every experience offers a mirror for how we perceive and interpret life. The deeper question is this: *Am I viewing this moment through the lens of the limited ego mind or through the larger, expanded awareness of love?* The invitation is to change your thinking, not your circumstances. This practice helps you discern which mindset is shaping your perception of the world. We are always seeing through one of two lenses—love (heaven) or fear (hell).

The practice of *The Questions*, provided at the end of this chapter, is the practice I use most frequently. I return to it often. Especially when I find myself struggling, caught in self-doubt, or awake in the middle of the night, moving through shame or fear without realizing how tightly it has gripped me. These questions work not because they offer a formula or a set of answers, but because they gently guide you back to truth—to a clearer, more grounded state of mind. At its heart, this practice is simply a path back to yourself. What the questions do first is invite openness. Then, almost immediately, they reveal the fearful mindset for what it is. Rather than forcing surrender, the practice then allows you to rest in the care of God—or Source, or love, however you name it. From that place, you begin to see what fear is actually doing. Fear is not love. It does not unify; it separates. And when fear loosens its grip, you are able to wait, to listen, and to see from a state of mind rooted in love. That is what these questions make possible.

Over time, you'll begin to see just how much your thinking shapes your reality. And you'll discover the power of simply noticing. Because when a thought is seen, it begins to lose its grip. With practice, you'll find more stillness in the mind, more clarity in the moment, and more space to respond with awareness instead of reacting from habit. This is beyond positive thinking. It's about thinking truthfully. It's about learning to hear your soul again, to remember who you are beneath the noise. You are not your thoughts. You are the one who listens. And in that space of listening, your true life begins to take shape.

Meditative Practice

- Dawnos *Disoriented* Album // Track 1 - The Questions
- Dawnos *Disoriented* Album // Track 2 - Voice of Love
- Dawnos *Disoriented* Album // Track 3 - Focus Point

Action Steps

1. Which recurring thought feels the most limiting right now?
2. Is this thought based on present truth or on a past story?
3. What belief might this thought be protecting or hiding?
4. What is one new thought you could practice as an anchor this week?

THE QUESTIONS

A TOOL TO HELP YOU CHANGE THE WAY YOU THINK ABOUT YOUR CIRCUMSTANCES

1. **Am I open to seeing or hearing this differently?**
2. **Is this a mind of fear or the mind of Love?**
3. **Am I willing to be in the care of Love?**
4. **What happens when I listen or see from a mind of fear?**
   (What images/messages of past or future, emotions, thoughts occur?)
5. **What does the mind of Love say or show?**

6

Emotions

"No feeling is final." - Rilke

It was Super Bowl Sunday, a few years after my divorce, a season when my weekends were devoted entirely to my children. I had my kids almost every weekend, which left little space for solitude. My weekdays were full of work and clients, and the weekends were filled with parenting. It was what I wanted, but in the midst of it, I rarely found time to be alone. That particular Sunday night, after dropping my kids off with their mother, I made a decision I hadn't made before. I packed a few things, got in the truck, and drove up into the hills of Tennessee to go backpacking for a couple of nights. I remember listening to the Super Bowl on the radio as I made my way there; Tom Brady's incredible comeback against the Falcons that night. I arrived late, parked my truck, set up camp, and settled in for the night. The next day, I hiked out to a stunning overlook—a wide, open vista where I set up my hammock right on the edge. It was only mid-afternoon, around three o'clock, and with camp set, there was nothing left to do. And then something surfaced.

As I sat there, completely alone, a familiar but unsettling feeling crept in. It was a kind of terror, not panic, but something deeper. I suddenly became aware of how much I had been insulated from this very moment by the constant motion of my life. Work, clients, kids: always something filling the space. But here, in the quiet, there was no one to tend to, no task to occupy my mind. And now, I was face-to-face with myself. The emptiness felt unbearable. For a while, I tried to bargain with myself. I calculated how long it would take to pack up and hike back to my truck. If I left soon, I could get back by dark, drive to Nashville, stop at Cracker Barrel for some comfort food, and sleep in my own bed. The temptation to run from the stillness was strong. But somewhere inside, I knew that if I left, I wouldn't just be leaving the campsite, I'd be running from myself. So I stayed.

And then it came. A wave of grief, raw and overwhelming, flooded me. I buckled under its weight, sobbing uncontrollably. I couldn't even name exactly what I was grieving. It was simply pain; unprocessed, unspoken, and now uncontainable. The waves came and went, gradually softening. What at first felt unbearable began to ease. And then came the release. The very thing I had feared, the grief itself, became the gift; the opening and the catharsis. In allowing myself to fully feel it, I found peace. What I had resisted became sacred ground. The evening that followed was calm, quiet, and a sense of ease. And now, years later, I look back on that moment not as one of pain, but almost as a moment of gratitude, a kind of strange glory that has stayed with me ever since.

The Practice - Reclaiming Your Emotional Life - Growing in Capacity

This module is about building emotional capacity, the ability to sit with what you feel without being overtaken by it. It's about learning to meet your emotions not as enemies or overwhelming forces, but as intelligent signals that carry messages from your heart. You are not your emotions. And yet, emotions live within you. They move through you. They are here to teach you something. The word emotion comes from the Latin *emovere*, meaning "to move." Emotions are meant to move us; but only if we allow them to be felt, named, and understood. When ignored or suppressed, emotions become blocked energy. They distort how we see ourselves, how we relate to others, and how we experience life.

In this module, we begin welcoming our emotions as guests, inviting them in, listening to them, and letting them speak without letting them take over. Each emotion carries a task, a gift, and an invitation:

- **Joy** invites connection.
- **Fear** invites courage, trust, and with it an alertness.
- **Passion** invites movement and purpose.
- **Sadness** invites grief and release, bringing depth.
- **Shame** invites self-love and repair.
- **Guilt** invites responsibility and restoration.
- **Anger** invites truth and redirection.
- **Loneliness** invites reconnection with self, others, and Source.

What begins to emerge is a new relationship to feeling. We stop resisting our emotional landscape and begin to see it as sacred ground. We become less reactive and more responsive. We no longer seek to be rescued from our feelings, but instead, we allow them to lead us back home. A core part of this process is learning to recognize needs without demanding they be fulfilled by others. Needs for validation, connection, safety, or touch are human. But when we expect others to meet these needs without first understanding them ourselves, we create entrapment. When we own our needs, express them vulnerably, and meet them from within, we discover a deeper freedom.

There is a simple emotional processing cycle we'll begin to practice:

1. **Identify** what you're feeling
2. **Notice the need** behind the emotion
3. **Accept** it without judgment
4. **Dissolve** through presence, breath, and compassion

This is how energy moves and emotions shift. This is how we grow in capacity: not by avoiding, but by staying, feeling, and softening.

As you begin to welcome your full emotional self, you reclaim your power. You gain the freedom to feel fully without spiraling. You stop demanding that others meet your emotional needs and instead bring that awareness into your own presence. And paradoxically, when you do this, when you stop grasping, those needs are often met more naturally, because they're no longer rooted in scarcity. They are shared, not demanded. This is the work of emotional maturity. It's quiet, courageous, and deeply healing. It frees you, and in turn, it frees the people around you. And as the poet Rilke said, "No feeling is final." If there's one essential truth to grasp, it's this: we are not responsible for the emotions that arise; they simply come. While we cannot control which emotions show up, we can learn to meet them differently and choose how we respond. And remember, we are not our emotions.

Meditative Practice

- Dawnos *Disoriented* Album // Track 4 - Emotional Cycle
- Dawnos *Disoriented* Album // Track 5 - Emotional Mastery
- Dawnos *Disoriented* Album // Track 6 - Capacity

Action Steps

1. What emotion do you avoid feeling the most?
2. What early experience or learned pattern shaped how you handle this emotion?
3. What is one safe way you can practice feeling it without judgment?
4. Will you practice sitting with that feeling today?

EMOTIONAL CYCLE

EMOTIONAL INFLAMMATION, COMPLETING THE EMOTIONAL CYCLE

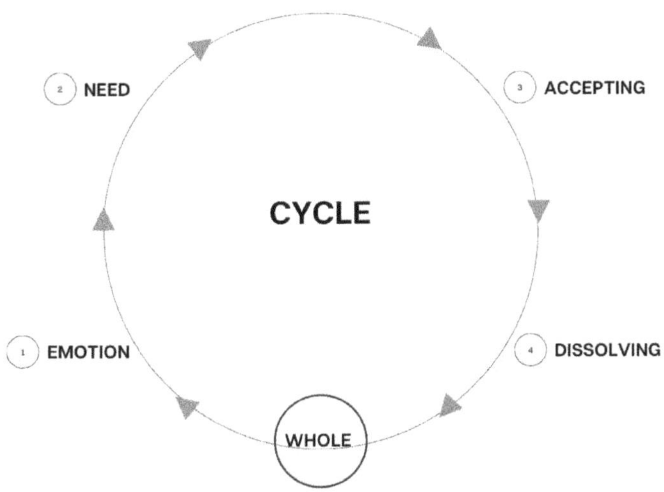

7

Smaller Self

"It is never too late to have a happy childhood." — Tom Robbins

There was a middle-aged man who, growing up, dreamed of being a songwriter. From an early age, he was a deep-feeler, a creative, someone drawn to creative expression through words, through music, through storytelling. But the world around him told a different story. He grew up in a buttoned-up home. Both his parents were accountants, professionals who valued stability, predictability, and security. In that environment, the idea of pursuing a creative path felt reckless, irresponsible, even foolish. He wasn't surrounded by artists or dreamers; creativity was not part of his family's language. And so, like many of us, he chose what felt responsible. He attended a prestigious college that aligned with his parents' vision, entered banking and finance, married, built a beautiful home, and raised wonderful children. From the outside, it looked like he had everything. Yet inside, there was an ache—a quiet but growing sense of inauthenticity. He wasn't fully living from who he truly was.

At 40, the weight of that inner divide caught up with him. He fell into a deep depression, which eventually led him to therapy. There, he reconnected with the younger version of himself, the boy he once was at five, six, and eight years old; full of dreams, imagination, and possibility. Alongside this rediscovery, he also met another voice within: the inner loving parent—a wise, compassionate guide who gently invited him to finally honor his creative call. With the support of his family, some savings, and a great deal of fear, he made the bold decision to leave his stable life behind. He moved to Nashville to pursue songwriting. It was a leap of faith. The risk was real. But the bigger risk, he realized, was staying disconnected from his soul.

And slowly, success did come, but that wasn't the point. What brought him peace was not external accomplishment but internal alignment. He was finally living true to who he was. And that's the invitation for all of us. Often, the smaller self whispers the lie that playing it safe is responsible. But there's a deeper responsibility, to listen to the call within. To step forward not recklessly, but faithfully. Not to abandon reason, but to honor the part of us that knows when it's time to risk for the sake of the soul.

The Practice – Returning to Second Innocence - Over-Identification with the Separate (Smaller) Self –

This module is about the slow, sacred work of integration. The task here is to remember who you've always been beneath the protective masks, the performance, the fear. It's about recognizing that the parts of you you've rejected or disowned, your insecurities, your survival patterns, your pain, were never meant to be cast out. They were waiting to be seen, heard, and nurtured.

We call this the *smaller self*. The personality you shaped in response to wounds, absence, or unmet needs. It's the version of you built to survive, not to thrive. And while it helped you navigate the world, it also placed limits on your joy, connection, and sense of worth. At the heart of this module is the realization that your wounds are not the opposite of your gift—they are the very soil from which it can grow. What you have tried to forget, suppress, or control might become the doorway to your deepest wisdom.

As children, many of us learned to split off parts of ourselves, to hide what wasn't accepted, to perform, to shrink, to fit. However, every split comes with a cost: disconnection from oneself, from the Source, and from others. The masks we wear begin to feel like the truth. The pain we suppress creates trance states of anxiety, shame, and fear. But the trance isn't reality, it's just a story held together by unexamined wounds.

And there comes a moment, a *wall,* when you know you are loved, but you don't feel it. When the practice isn't "working." This is the turning point. You are on the edge of transformation, though it can be very uncomfortable. The breakthrough lives just beyond this numbness. And the path through it is not one of control or striving, but gentle and consistent nurturing. This is where the Inner Loving Parent comes in: a voice of Love that interrupts the ego's self-criticism and shame. Instead of trying to fix, it simply loves. And through that connection, correction happens naturally. To support this, we use the PARENT Tool:

a step-by-step practice to help you re-parent and integrate fragmented parts of yourself. Here's how it works:

The PARENT Tool is a way to intervene in those moments when we slip into trance, often unknowingly, and begin reacting from an old, conditioned place. It offers a gentle, step-by-step path inward. First, you identify what you're thinking and feeling, recognizing this as a part of you rather than the whole of you. You notice where this experience lives in your body and begin to inquire with curiosity rather than judgment. Then comes a crucial turn: you look back and ask when you have felt this way before. As the saying goes in therapeutic circles, "If it's hysterical, it's historical." What feels overwhelming in the present is often rooted in an unconscious childhood moment that is resurfacing—not to torment you, but to be healed. From here, the work deepens. You imagine an ideal, loving environment and invite in your adult self, or an inner loving parent, to offer presence, reassurance, and care. In doing so, you open access to the inner voice of love. As this happens, the body begins to respond. The energy shifts. What was once contracted often softens into warmth, connection, and a quiet sense of wholeness.

This process may seem small, but it is sacred. It's how we rewrite the old script. It's how we begin to see ourselves not as broken or wrong, but as worthy, whole, and in progress. The inner child is the divine spark within you that never stopped believing, loving, and hoping. Reconnecting to that part of yourself isn't regression; it's resurrection. It's what we call second innocence, a conscious return to your original essence, a profound sense of awareness, compassion, and strength. You do not need to reject your past to move forward. You need to welcome it with love. The very parts of you that feel broken may become your brilliance. A healer once told me, "If it's in the way, it is the way." What obstructs us is often the very path forward. And so, the invitation in this module is simple, but radical:

- Everything belongs, even the shadow—especially the shadow.
- Your inner child is caught in the past, waiting to be loved and integrated.
- You are already what you've been looking for.

This is the work of wholeness. This is the path home. Remember, we are not our story (i.e., our separate, smaller self), and yet it is part of us.

Meditative Practice

- Dawnos *Disoriented* Album // Track 7 - Inner Child
- Dawnos *Disoriented* Album // Track 8 - Nurturing Figure
- Dawnos *Disoriented* Album // Track 9 - PARENT

Action Steps

1. When you feel triggered, what younger version of yourself might be showing up?
2. What story from that time still influences how you react today?
3. What would it look like to meet that part of yourself with compassion instead of criticism?

PARENT

A TOOL TO HELP REPARENT YOURSELF AND INTEGRATE SPLIT PARTS OF YOU BACK TO SELF

P	PART	Identify the part of you that is feeling distress, the emotions, the thoughts, etc.
A	ASK	Access/Ask/Analyze where you are feeling it in your body. Allow yourself to fully connect to this part of you.
R	REMEMBER	Recall a childhood moment, noticing what was left unfinished or what you needed but didn't receive. Picture yourself there, and gently connect with your younger self.
E	ENVISION	Imagine an ideal childhood environment—one truly suited to you. Picture the nurturing figures you needed, noticing their qualities, care, and how they would relate to you.
N	NURTURE	Notice these loving parental qualities being shown to you, especially in the places that have felt painful or unmet. Then imagine your adult self offering that same care to this part of you.
T	TRANSFORM	Wait for an Alchemy to occur. This energy will dissolve. The intensity will lessen.

8

Grief

"The only cure for grief is grief itself." – David Whyte

The day I told my father that my first marriage was ending marked one of the most significant thresholds of my life. For over a year, I had wrestled in silence, sitting in the I don't know, caught in the ache of grief, uncertainty, and struggle. I didn't have clarity, only questions and the quiet unraveling of what I thought life was supposed to be.

That evening, I drove to my father's home and sat across from him, heavy with the weight of what I needed to say. After I told him about the divorce, he paused for a long moment, then looked at me and said softly, "James, allow for the unfolding." Then he began to recite a poem I had once given him, one we had both read often. Thomas Merton's The Serene Disciple, found at the end of Richard Rohr's Falling Upward[6]. The words landed differently that night:

"When stars as well as friends are angry with the noble ruin,
saints depart in several directions...
It is a lucky sea that drowned his reputation,
a lucky wind that blew his halo with his cares...
What choice remains to be ordinary is not a choice,
it is the usual freedom." - Thomas Merton, "The Serene Disciple"

Merton's lines spoke of a quiet surrender, the kind that comes when the first half of life begins to die and the second half begins to stir. My father's invitation was to allow the life I had known to dissolve, making room for something deeper and truer to emerge. Grief became my teacher that night. It was an acknowledgment of *the initiation*, an invitation into the cave, to let go of what was no longer mine and to trust the unfolding mystery of what was becoming.

As I've reflected on grief and searched for the right words, I've come to see that grief may be the one experience we can never fully describe. As much as it has been said before, it remains true that each person's grief is uniquely their own. Perhaps that is why it resists language. There is no single moment, no singular narrative, that can carry the full weight of its depth.

In many ways, there are no words. Only these small, imperfect attempts to name the experience. Grief gathers heartbreak, disorientation, longing, fear, and love, folding them into a kind of vortex that few of us know how to navigate. And truthfully, who would choose to? Who longs to walk through grief? And yet, all I can say is this: it's an unspeakable undoing that, somehow, we each encounter in our own way. It is never glorious in the beginning. There's no ease in its arrival. While there may be a temptation to run, numb, or spiritually bypass, if we allow ourselves to stay with it, something begins to soften. And though it may sound dangerously close to cliché, I believe this: on the other side of grief, there is a kind of quiet transformation. Something shifts and opens. What once felt only like loss becomes, in its own strange way, a form of grace.

The Practice - Entering the Unknown by Exploring Your Grief

Grief does not ask for permission before it arrives. It often moves in like a storm; unpredictable, disorienting, and absolute. One day, life is ordered, known, familiar. And then, suddenly, it is not. Something precious is gone. Someone, some version of you, some hope or dream, lost. And there is no going back. This is the threshold, the initiation into the unknown.

Grief drops us squarely into what I call the season of disorientation, the middle space between being oriented (when life felt stable and predictable) and being reoriented (when a new sense of meaning begins to take form). In disorientation, the entrance into grief is fully invoked: a state of groundlessness, free fall, or what some call the Shadowlands. It can feel as though you're picking up the pieces after your own personal disaster; lost, fractured, unsure if you will ever find solid ground again.

And yet, much like chaos theory suggests, there is a hidden order within the chaos. We just can't see it yet. It's moving beneath the surface, working in the deep, unlit chambers of the subconscious where transformation quietly takes root. Richard Rohr describes this progression as order, disorder, and reorder; another way to say it is to be oriented to a dream or expectation, then disordered, and finally reoriented toward a new vision, often one much larger, deeper, and more authentic than before.

Disorientation is unsettling, confusing, and at times unbearable. But it's also essential to transformation. The old orientation must dissolve before the new one can emerge. This is grief's true work—not rushing to rebuild, but remaining in the space where everything feels undone, trusting that this groundlessness is the soil in which the seeds of a new life are being sown. In this space, there are no quick fixes, no polished answers. Encouragement may fall flat. Advice often makes it worse. And silence may feel like the only companion who understands. Grief is not a problem to solve; it is a passage to walk and live slowly and with reverence. This is the cave that every wisdom tradition speaks of, the dark womb of transformation. Also known as the dark night of the soul. The place where identity dissolves, and the soul is reshaped. When we resist it, we suffer more. When we surrender to it, something shifts and deepens.

At first, it may feel like nothing but loss. And truthfully, it is; loss of a person, a life, a dream, an old identity. But there's something else beneath the ache. A quiet thread of becoming. Something you can't name but can feel. If you stay long enough, the work of grief is not to return to the life you had before. It's to let go of what is no longer there, so that something more expansive can emerge. It is neither linear nor efficient. It is a holy unraveling, though it feels anything but holy. It will feel cruel.

And in this unraveling, you will confront your shadow. Your fears, your beliefs about abandonment, shame, and unworthiness. You'll hear the old voices rise up: you should be over this. You're too much, and you're alone. But here's the truth: you are not your pain. You are not your fear. These are weather patterns, not definitions. Let them move through you, not define you.

This is a time for courage, not the kind that conquers, but the kind that sits with what's hard and doesn't flinch. The kind that stays open, even in darkness. The kind that whispers, *"I don't know what's next, but I won't abandon myself here."* Grief strips us down, but it doesn't leave us empty. It makes room. It expands the vessel. In time, it grows your capacity to feel, to hold, to love more deeply. And this becomes the alchemy. Grief doesn't just end. It transforms and shapes you into someone more whole, more tender, more real. You don't have to understand it. You just have to enter it. Let yourself grieve and be undone. And trust, quietly and fiercely, that what feels like the end may be the beginning of a deeper you. It is time to enter the cave. But just know the ember of your soul is still burning.

Meditative Practice

- Dawnos *Disoriented* Album // Track 10 - Parts Integration
- Dawnos *Disoriented* Album // Track 11 - Cocoon
- Dawnos *Disoriented* Album // Track 12 - Smile

Action Steps

1. What loss or change are you being asked to acknowledge right now?
2. How have you been avoiding grief?
3. What is one small way you can honor what you've lost?
4. What practice will you do to sit with grief?

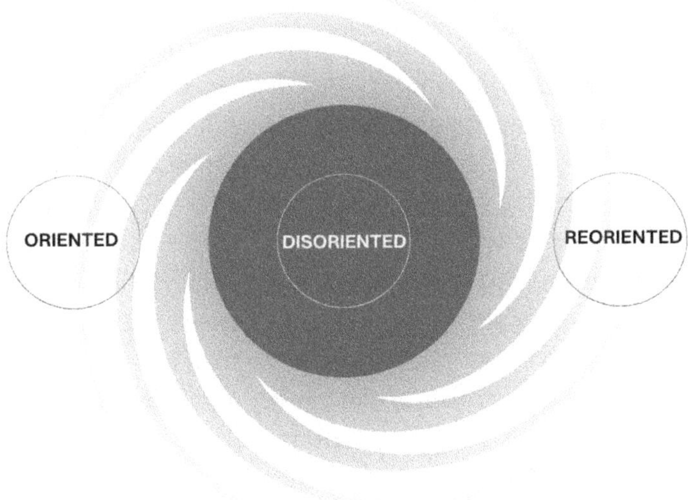

9

Powerlessness

"You do not need to know where you are going, provided you know that God knows." — *Thomas Merton*

Several years after my divorce, I went through what I can only describe as a dark night of the soul—a season marked by profound grief and disorientation. It began with my mother's passing. Around that same time, Mary and I, who had been dating for about a year and a half, decided to take a break. We weren't married yet, but the love was unlike anything I had known before, and the separation felt like another massive loss. Not long after, I moved from Nashville to Chattanooga to be closer to my children. And in the span of a few months, everything I had dreamed and worked to rebuild seemed to dissolve. There was a deep, almost brutal sense of letting go. I didn't understand what was happening.

In many ways, it mirrored the grief I felt after my brother Mark's death, twenty years earlier, of that same ache and bewilderment. And yet, beneath all of it, I still carried a quiet, almost irrational belief that Mary and I would somehow find our way back to each other. It felt like a wild hope; part belief, part disbelief. But I knew that if it was going to happen, it couldn't come through my effort. It had to come through her reaching out. That would be the sign. And so, for three years, I lived with an unrelenting hope and vision, an ache that invited me into the strange posture of faith grief sometimes demands. I even tried to move on. There were seasons where I felt like I had let Mary go. But she would inevitably come back to my mind with longing that didn't make sense, and a hope that wouldn't go away. After all, Mary was in Nashville, and I was in Chattanooga. I questioned myself constantly about this longing. Was I deluding myself? Was this some kind of fantasy I needed to let go of?

But I couldn't shake it. The vision of reconciliation stayed with me, often in my subconscious, and it kept resurfacing, much to my dismay. So much so that at times I wondered if something was wrong with me. I could almost hear my friends saying, "Dude, just get over her," or maybe that was simply my inner critic speaking. It felt like madness. And yet, something deeper kept whispering: just stay open. My father's words never left me: "Watch the unfolding. It's all in the unfolding, James." And Cookie, a second mother to me, would say, "Don't close your heart and be surprised. It is going to blow you away." At the time, I did not fully believe that love would be with Mary. But sure enough, three years later, Mary happened to hear my voice on a song a friend of mine had recorded. That is when she reached out, we reconnected, started dating again, and a year and a half later, we were married. That season taught me the power of waiting, though not perfectly, and yet a deeper path and undercurrent were in motion. Something beyond what I could have imagined or controlled. A mentor of mine, Barbara, once told me, "You don't have to find it. It finds you. You don't have to figure it out. It figures you out. Just keep your heart open to love." This is that stage.

The Practice - Opening to Powerlessness

There comes a point on the path where nothing seems to move; not forward, not backward. The grief has quieted, but the clarity hasn't returned. You're not where you were, but you're not yet where you're going. This is the space of powerlessness, though it can feel like a purgatory without end. It is a threshold. Here, the soul asks for surrender over solutions, for stillness over striving. You may feel like you're in free fall; disoriented, unmoored, stripped of direction or purpose. This is the dissolving of the smaller self, the ego's loosening grip. What once guided you no longer applies. What once gave meaning no longer fits. And so, you're asked to sit, to stay, and to listen. Powerlessness invites and teaches you to be present without control. It's the space where the "third way" begins to appear; not the grasping of the fight reaction, nor the avoidance of the flight response. But something else entirely. It is a quiet allowing and surrender. A trust that rises in the space, the gap, where mystery is the newfound friend. The third way doesn't arrive through effort. It finds you when you stop trying to escape.

Your shadow will rise here, asking to be seen. It may feel like self-sabotage or a haunting presence, but that interpretation does not tell the whole story. This long-rejected, long-misunderstood part of you carries wisdom, reflection, and guidance. Integration is the path forward. The work is to understand what it's protecting and to ask what it's pointing toward. There is a wisdom in the dark, one that doesn't shout. It waits, whispers, and offers depth under the surface. And in this silence, something begins to form. It creates the capacity to hold more, beyond the old clinging. What emerges is a new way of being that doesn't need to prove or push. It is a reorientation from doing to being.

In this space, you come to know stillness as power. Stillness sharpens your ability to see, hear, and choose. In a sense, an antenna has now been raised. It transforms everyday moments into sacred ones. It shifts your mode of action to that of alignment. The tyranny of the urgent dissolves. And then comes the paradox: you are not actually powerless. You have power far deeper than the ego can imagine. The power to choose presence, love, and the ability to stay on your path. Even here, especially here, your soul has not abandoned you. It has never been closer. The task is to be open.

This open practice, outlined in the chart at the end of the chapter, is a practical way to process emotions and foster integration. At its core, the practice invites a shift into the observer, the Larger Self. Rather than remaining bound to the smaller self, caught in the old trance of overidentifying with our thoughts or emotions, stillness creates the capacity to step back and witness what is happening within us. From this place of observation, we enter flow, and acceptance is established. We give ourselves permission to be with the energy rather than resist it. And it is precisely this openness that gives us the depth and capacity to explore what is unfolding in the body, the heart, and the mind. As understanding emerges, we begin to know how to nurture ourselves back into wholeness. This statement by Louis Cozolino says it beautifully, "It is not the survival of the fittest, but the survival of the nurtured."

This is the narrow way, the liminal space where what was falls away and what is becoming is gently formed and becomes clearer. Even though it is not a straight line or immediate, it is real. Here, letting go is no longer a loss. It is a return. You begin to realize that what you feared losing was never who you were to begin with. And what remains: the tiny ember, the unnameable peace, that is you, shines forth. That is what you've been searching for all along. Let the stillness work on you. Let the silence say what words cannot. Trust the alchemy because something beautiful is taking shape.

Meditative Practice

- Dawnos *Reoriented* Album // Track 1 - Unknown
- Dawnos *Reoriented* Album // Track 2 - OPEN
- Dawnos *Reoriented* Album // Track 3 - Shadow Boxing

Action Steps

1. Where are you still trying to force an outcome?
2. What pattern, past experience, or belief makes it hard to release control?
3. What would it mean to sit in this space without rushing to a solution?
4. Will you practice using the OPEN meditation several times this week?

OPEN

A TOOL TO HELP CONNECT TO THE NEGATIVE ENERGY AND STATE IN ORDER TO SHIFT

O	OBSERVE IT	Feel the emotions, notice the thoughts, and the story you are thinking and believing.
P	PERMISSION	Rather than resist the energy, try to allow it to be here, engage it.
E	EXPLORE	Inquire the following in the body: Location, Shape, Weight, Color, Temperature, Age (younger self).
N	NURTURE	Allow yourself to merge with the energy, become one with it, nurture yourself through it.

10

Larger Self

"Don't ask what the world needs. Ask what makes you come alive, and go do it. Because what the world needs is people who have come alive." —Howard Thurman

During that three-year stretch, after I moved to Chattanooga, I began settling into a new rhythm of life. I had shifted my practice out of Nashville, and in doing so, I opened space to read, write, and create. One of the things that happened during that season was that I picked up a book: The Artist's Way. It introduced me to a practice called morning pages[7]—waking up each morning and writing, nonstop, stream-of-consciousness, for about an hour. And something began to happen. This inner voice, quiet at first, started to grow louder. I began to notice there were actually two voices inside me. One was familiar: the voice of fear, self-doubt, second-guessing. But the other was different. It was gentler. It was the dreamer. It was the part of me that had vision, that imagined possibilities, that whispered risk. And it kept saying: Write. Keep writing. And then, unexpectedly, it said something else: "You need to start recording meditations." Put them to music. Create the thing you've always imagined.

Now, this was strange. I had no formal musical background. I had friends connected to the Nashville music scene, but this felt...far-fetched. A little reckless and way out there. But the voice didn't stop. It kept urging: Do it. This is part of your path. You've always wanted to do this. And then something happened—something completely outside of my plans. My close friend Judah Akers, of Judah and the Lion, recorded one of my meditations from an interview I'd done with him and his bandmate Brian MacDonald. Without any effort or expectation on my part, they included it on The Process album, as an interlude called "Bargaining[8]". And that was the song Mary heard.

It was a confirmation. The truth is, it all came from those morning pages. That daily act of writing became an opening, a widening, a gateway to something deeper. Here's what I learned: If we're taught to doubt that deep inner voice: if we're conditioned by culture, by church, or by fear to distrust the very part of us that dreams, that creates, that longs—then what's left to guide us? What stabilizes us if we no longer believe in the voice within? If we can't trust that voice... whose voice are we following? Many of us have been told that pursuing our passion is selfish or misguided. But if we're not following what's uniquely ours to do, then who, or what, are we following? That voice, what I've come to understand as the larger self, was trying to speak. And when I finally gave it space, it said, "Go create the thing you're here to create." It's not reckless to follow that voice. It's reckless not to.

The Practice - Living from Your Larger Self

This module marks an arrival, not the end, but the beginning of a new way of living. You've walked through grief, surrendered to powerlessness, and now you begin to live from something deeper. This is your larger self, not a version of you shaped by fear or external expectations, but the one that has always existed underneath: whole, clear, connected, and good. At this stage, the voice within begins to lead. It's not the loud, anxious voice of the ego, but the quiet, steady voice of truth. Your task now is to trust it. This inner voice is intuitive, loving, and deeply connected to your Source. It's the voice that gently says: *You can be trusted. You know the way.* Instead of forcing life forward, you begin to let life move through you. What once felt like effort becomes flow.

Here you arrive at a reorientation, when the hidden order of the chaos begins to reveal itself. What once felt like meaningless disarray now begins to take shape, like a puzzle in which the edges suddenly appear, giving context to the scattered pieces. The free fall slows. Ground reappears beneath your feet, though it may feel new and unfamiliar. Then somehow you land on your feet. The vision you carried before—the dream, the plan, the identity—has been broken open and re-formed into something larger and truer. Much like chaos theory teaches, what felt random and destructive was part of a deeper pattern, one that the subconscious has been quietly weaving the whole time. In the disorientation stage, this order was invisible; now it begins to emerge into view. You realize you've been changed, not by avoiding the chaos, but by passing through it. This new orientation isn't a return to the way things were; it's a step into a life infused with greater clarity, humility, and purpose. What felt like the end was, all along, the beginning of a new way of being.

As a result, there is a radical shift in how you perceive your inner world. The thoughts, emotions, and reactions of your ego self don't disappear, but they no longer occupy center stage. They move to the background. The foreground view now brings presence, clarity, joy, stillness, and purpose. You begin to live from the calm center of your being, no longer reacting to life, but responding and *creating* from your essence. This is what it means to embody your larger self. You'll notice that gratitude becomes a powerful tool in this stage. When things arise, whether joy or challenge, you're learning to shift perspective and ask: *What is this showing me?* Even difficult emotions become gateways to insight. From this openness, a muse begins to emerge. This is your inner genius, your creative spirit, your channel to Source. It flows more freely now, not because you forced it, but because you stepped out of the way.

As you trust this voice and move from this center, you'll begin to notice how the people you admire or feel drawn to reflect your own inner qualities. This mirroring is not a coincidence; it's a clue. The strength, creativity, or clarity you see in others is already alive in you, ready to be fully expressed. You'll face a choice every day: return to the old ways of living small, or walk forward into your unique expression. This is the heroic task, not to chase purpose, but to live it. To let the dreams inside you rise without shame or apology. To believe that what you've been given is not only real, it's meant to be shared. Over time, your life energy reorients, rooted in positivity rather than despair. This is the deep shadow work of allowing the darkness to teach us.

The practice of the HOPE Tool is anything but spiritual bypass. Spiritual bypassing relies on forced positivity, an attempt to skip over pain or fake one's way through suffering. HOPE, as it's practiced here, does the opposite. It embraces the full humanity of life: the struggles, the hard knocks, and the tragedies that inevitably come. It does not turn away from the emotional, physical, and at times brutal cuts that life can bring. Instead, it moves directly toward them. And in that honest embracing, something begins to open. This openness to what is, not what we wish were different, allows us, over time, to arrive at a deeper truth. Everything is as it should be. On the front end of grief, that truth can feel impossible, even offensive. How could this be as it should be? But through the lived process of grief, something shifts. We don't arrive at approval or justification; we arrive at acceptance. I know this personally in the loss of my brother, Mark. While I wish it had never happened, I can also say I am grateful for what has been revealed through the grief. It is what it is. And that is peace. From this place, a wider awareness emerges, a felt sense of interconnectedness, of belonging to something larger than ourselves. We begin to sense a deeper intelligence at work, a larger unfolding beyond our finite minds' grasp. HOPE, then, is not denial. It is the courage to stay present long enough for truth to reveal itself.

You return now to your original innocence, not naïve or unaware, but grounded in wisdom. You see with new eyes, hear with deeper trust, and live from a broader horizon. What once felt like a struggle has shaped you into someone more expansive, more rooted, and more alive. This is not about striving to become someone else. This is about remembering who you are and allowing your life to rise from that knowing, connected to what is real.

Meditative Practice

- Dawnos *Reoriented* Album // Track 4 - Cosmic Hum
- Dawnos *Reoriented* Album // Track 5 - New View
- Dawnos *Reoriented* Album // Track 6 - HOPE

Action Steps

1. What is one area of life where you feel most aligned with your deeper self?
2. What patterns or fears still pull you back toward the smaller self?
3. What creative expression or act of service could you step into from this place of wholeness?

HOPE

A TOOL TO RECONNECT TO INNER STRENGTH BY HONORING YOUR EXPERIENCE AND OPENING TO POSSIBILITY.

H	HUMANITY	This involves fully embracing the entirety of our thoughts, emotions, and feelings. It is about experiencing the richness of life and allowing ourselves to fully engage in every moment.
O	OPEN	The pivot involves embracing the vastness and expansiveness that lies beyond oneself. It means opening yourself to the broader world that exists beyond your individual perspective and experience.
P	PEACE	With this shift, you embrace the notion of "it is as it should be," and a profound sense of peace begins to emerge.
E	EVERYTHING	At this ultimate juncture, the understanding that you are intertwined with everything, and that everything is intertwined with you, becomes a profound realization.

11

Connection

"We are the sum of all our parts." — Thomas Wolfe

There is a story, not found in any single tradition, but echoing through many, that we each begin whole, and over time, become scattered. Not by accident, but through experience. Through pain, through growth, through forgetting. And then, at some point, often much later, we begin the long walk home to ourselves.

I've often imagined that inner journey like stepping into a mythical land—something between Narnia and the subconscious, where memory becomes terrain and emotion becomes weather. In this place, the landscape shifts with each step. One moment you're in a frozen forest of silence and withdrawal, the next in a desert of shame, or a meadow touched by forgotten joy. Nothing is static, and everything mirrors something from your story. Here, scattered across the terrain, are the parts of you that went missing. The brave one who stood up for what mattered. The lover who felt deeply and wasn't afraid to say so. The protector, the dreamer, the inner child, even the shadow, the part you've tried to exile or ignore. Each one waits in a particular corner of this inner world, shaped by the relationships, memories, and moments that formed them. And the work, your sacred work, is to find them. To face the challenge of re-entering the terrain that shaped their exile. To move through resistance, emotion, and fear. And then, gently, to welcome them back.

In this kind of integration, something begins to shift. Each lost part doesn't just return as it once was; it returns transformed. What was once a burden becomes a form of strength. What once frightened you reveals its hidden wisdom. And with every reunion, you grow not only in understanding, but in presence, in capacity, in wholeness. You begin to feel it: the alchemy of inner healing. The slow merging of parts once split off, returning to the center of your being. But something else happens, too. As you come home to yourself, you begin to notice you're not just healing *inwardly.* You're changing how you move through the world. The more connected you are to your inner life, the more connected you feel to everything around you. The trees speak more clearly. The silence feels alive. You listen differently to the people you love. Even ordinary moments shimmer with meaning. It's not that life gets easier. It's that you stop resisting it.

And maybe this is what Jesus meant when he spoke of the one lost sheep being worth going after. Maybe the lost sheep is not someone else "out there". Maybe it's the part of *you* that wandered off in grief, or fear, or shame, and is now ready to be found.

The Practice - Connected + Flow

This is the return: a way of being, rather than a far-off place or destination, that is a home within yourself, a rhythm that feels both brand new and deeply familiar. Because it has been here all along, waiting for you to remember. After the thresholds, the disorientation, and the inner work that required everything of you, you arrive at a different kind of awareness. The ego's illusions begin to fall away. The haunted house no longer haunts. The prison door was never locked. What once felt like a constant fight—for peace, for clarity, for wholeness—is replaced by a quiet knowing. A sense that what you've been seeking has been seeking you.

Forgiveness flows now, creating the space to look at what once caused so much pain. You find that you seek to forgive because it is a natural release, and instead of recoiling, you feel a strange, sacred kind of gratitude. You see how it shaped you. You see how it brought you here. And with that, the flow begins. This is the moment love becomes rhythm. You receive it. You remember that you are it. And then, without trying, you give it. This giving doesn't deplete you. It energizes you. This love isn't forced. It's the overflow of a life finally aligned. There's a harmony now between your inner life and your outer actions. The vision you once dreamed of, way back at the beginning of this path, is no longer just a guiding light; it's a mission you're living. You've become the person your soul always believed you could be.

Connection is no longer about effort. It's about openness. You flow because you're no longer resisting. You rest because you've stopped performing. The very rhythm of life begins to feel like a stream you belong to, one that carries you forward with grace. You don't need to prove anything anymore. You don't need to be anyone else. You are here. You are whole. You are connected: to Source, to yourself, to the world. This is not the end of your journey, but it is the return to where it always begins. The garden, the sanctuary, the place inside you that never left. You've come home.

Here we begin to see our true mission: love and forgiveness. And it can be radical. In this forgiveness, the practice you will find in the meditation is tonglen, the movement of sending love where pain once landed. When attacks come, when assaults or negative energy move toward you, something has changed. The old self that clung to grudges, resentment, and projection, turning it all inward, no longer needs to hold any of it. Instead, you send love, and it's way beyond bypass or denial. It is a privilege. You discover that you do not have to carry what was never yours to begin with. You simply see the other person clearly. You breathe in their suffering, recognizing how stuck they are, and you breathe love back toward them. You see their fear. You see their shame. But it no longer sticks.

You are shielded by love. There is nothing left to defend because what we defend, we make real. When we are connected, there is no battle, only clarity. You can say, quietly and honestly, *I send you love. I love you.* Not as sentimentality, not as a cliché, but as truth. Because beneath it all, this is what remains. As Bono sings in U2's song One, "We are one, but not the same". And everything returns to love.

Meditative Practice

- Dawnos *Reoriented* Album // Track 7 - Flow
- Dawnos *Reoriented* Album // Track 8 - Tonglen
- Dawnos *Reoriented* Album // Track 9 - Gratitude

Action Steps

1. Will you set aside time this week to sit in stillness and simply notice what is—without trying to change it?
2. Will you take a few minutes to write down 20 things, people, or experiences you feel grateful for?
3. Will you practice "the third way" in a situation that normally triggers fight-or-flight, and simply be with the tension? (Consider using the Tonglen Meditation as a guide.)

THIRD WAY

FROM RESISTANCE TO FLOW—RECEIVE, INTEGRATE, RESPOND WITH LOVE.

Clinging or escalating often springs from anger and fear—the shadow of control that tries to force solutions from a power stance, reducing everything to right vs. wrong.

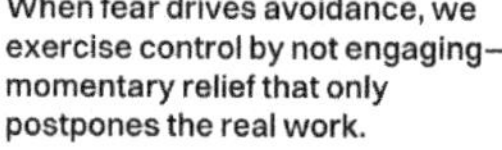

The third way receives the energy and softens it into peace and connection, releasing the demand for an immediate fix. From this stance—"everything is as it should be"—we let events unfold for ourselves and others, meeting what comes and working with it.

12

Wholeness

"I am not what happened to me, I am what I choose to become." — Carl Jung

Here is a story of a modern-day alchemist. I once worked with an older client who had recently retired. What struck me most about her wasn't what she had accomplished, but what she had released.

She told me, almost in passing, that her greatest joy these days came from simply enjoying who she was. She no longer cared about pleasing anyone. She didn't get pulled into other people's drama. She lived a quiet, unassuming life. Though she lived on a fixed income, she radiated contentment. She was no longer driven by the world's hollow promises of happiness or success. Somewhere along the way, she had found something richer, something real. And she had earned it. Earlier in life, she had endured profound trauma, abuse, abandonment, and the kind of emotional pain that could have easily shaped a bitter future. In midlife, depression and isolation took hold. There were years when she could barely find her footing and leave her house. But somehow, she didn't give up. She not only faced it, but also healed and transformed by connecting with her inner child. Little by little, the weight began to lift.

Now, in her late 60's, that pain felt like a faint shadow. She had come home to herself. She was active in her community, attended weekly gatherings, and mentored younger women seeking clarity. But she didn't rush in with advice. She simply shared her story. Her presence alone seemed to offer a kind of peace. She was fully at ease saying, *"I am who I am."* And that was enough. She had forgiven others. She had forgiven herself. In her own quiet way, she had become an alchemist, and instead of transforming metal into gold, she transformed suffering into wisdom. She helped others see their lives differently by sharing her own strength, hope, and love, thereby embodying wholeness. This is what it means to live from integration. This is what it means to return to the gold.

The Practice - Wholeness — "I Am Who I Am"

This is the homecoming. The return is more than a place; it is presence. Resting in the truth that you are already whole. You are the one you've been seeking. After all the unraveling, the thresholds, the grief, the releasing, the awakening, something quiet emerges: stillness. A peace that doesn't come from answers, but from presence itself. The pressure to strive, prove, or earn your place in the world has dissolved. You simply are. "I Am Who I Am" is more than a statement of identity; it is a declaration of reality. The ego's chasing has fallen away. Now, you live from ease, an overflow of *being.*

Wholeness is beyond perfection; it is inclusion. It means you've embraced your full humanity: your mistakes, your glory, your wounds, your gifts. You've made peace with your past and allowed joy to take up residence in your life, not as a visitor but as a native. You find that you can laugh at yourself. Gratitude, creativity, and play arise naturally, without force. You are now connected to your inner child, not as a forgotten fragment that once felt exiled. The inner child has been welcomed home. From this place, your soul begins to create for expression's sake and for the simple delight of participating in life's unfolding.

In this wholeness, a different kind of power emerges, the power to liberate. A quiet confidence takes root, grounded rather than egoic. There is a steadiness now, and a trust in the gentle guidance that has carried you here. You move through life with both softness and strength, aligned with something deeper and true. Nothing needs to be proved anymore. You know you are enough. Living from this place, there is no reason or need to reach beyond yourself for completion. Pain, past, and longing are met rather than avoided. You are here, and being here is enough. This is the shift: from grasping to being, from effort to embodiment, from fantasy to destiny, and from the idea of wholeness to its lived reality. You are who you are, and it is good to be you.

In this final practice, known as the PRESENT Tool, we arrive at the culmination of the full arc of The Holland Method. Here, presence is more than an idea; it is lived. You begin by noticing what you are seeing, because you now have the capacity to be present. You can see clearly. Through the practices that have come before, you have learned to discern whether your perception is arising from fear or from love. You can question whether what you are experiencing is reality or a false reality, and you can feel the difference in the body, between tightness and constriction, and a sense of wholeness and ease. You can see through the virtual reality of the smaller self. You have become attuned. You have awakened.

From this place, connection to Source is beyond any sacrifice or effort. It is an invitation because being in the care of love is not something to resist; it is something to enter. It becomes good to be in the body. It becomes safe to explore the energy you are holding. That energy is not something to avoid or endure; it becomes something you can move with, listen to, and be empowered by. You discover the capacity to nurture, embrace, and hold your experience, because you realize you are not alone. You are connected and surrounded by your own loving awareness and held by something larger than yourself.

From here, resources naturally emerge. You are able to wait for each moment, situation, and challenge to unfold and transform. And in time, something profound reveals itself: you are not waiting for the miracle. You are living as it is. Through forgiveness, you embody love. Through presence, you carry the light forward.

Meditative Practice

- Dawnos *Reoriented* Album // Track 10 - PRESENT
- Dawnos *Reoriented* Album // Track 11 - I Am
- Dawnos *Reoriented* Album // Track 12 - Alchemy

Action Steps

1. Do you like who you are? If not, what aspects of yourself do you not like? (Those aspects may point the way back.)
2. Can you write down three qualities that emerge when you feel most like yourself—and commit to embodying them today?
3. Where are you still searching outside yourself for validation? What might it look like to bring that search inward?

PRESENT

A TOOL INTEGRATING THE FULL RANGE OF THE HEALING PROCESS

P	PERCEIVE	Notice how you are seeing a troubling situation. Are you perceiving from a state of fear?
R	REALITY	Question if your perception is Reality. Is it true?
E	EXPERIENCE	Noticing how your Body is responding. Is it from the Ego's Body's perspective or Whole Body?
S	SOURCE	Invite in Help. Bring in Love, Support, Truth, and Peace.
E	EXPLORE	Become familiar with the Felt Sense of the energy you are holding.
N	NURTURE	Rather than resist the energy, try to allow it to be here, engage it. Nurture by merging with the energy. Learn to not resist it.
T	TRANSFORM	Wait for an Alchemy to occur. This energy will dissolve. The intensity will lessen.

Epilogue

Back on Thanksgiving 2024, I was riding my road bike with my father along the brow of Signal Mountain, a stretch of the plateau with incredible views. After the ride, we sat together in the kitchen drinking coffee, continuing a conversation that had started earlier during the ride. I had been sharing with him all the good things unfolding in my life. At that point, I was dating Mary, though we weren't married yet, but I felt a deep sense of possibility with her. There was excitement and hope, but also some nervousness about how things would unfold. Still, I could see all the reasons it could work, and I was holding that vision with care. I shared all of this with my father: the sense of new beginnings, especially after a long and difficult chapter—the previous 20 years marked by a hard first marriage, the challenges our kids had faced, the loss of my brother, and the passing of my mother after her battle with cancer. Somehow, it felt as if life were beginning to come back.

As we talked, another memory surfaced. The day I learned about my brother's death, I had gone on a trail run in Carmel, California. At the time, I had been studying the Book of Job. I remember thinking that my life had been so good that I couldn't truly understand what Job had gone through, or what it would be like to lose so much. Later that afternoon, I got the call about my brother's suicide. I recalled this moment to my father, and said, "You know, the story of Job is about restoration, right? That everything is ultimately returned."

But my father paused and looked at me. "That's not how I interpret Job," he said. Surprised, I asked, "Then what do you think it means?" He quoted Job 42:2: "No purpose of mine can be thwarted." Then he said it in simpler terms. "It is what it is. Job was at peace with what is."

That stopped me. I realized that the true peace Job found wasn't in restoring what was lost, but in the radical acceptance of *life as it is*. That's where the shift happened. The older life tried to force, fix, or recreate. But in an expanded life, you flow with it. This is the essence of transformation: the alchemy of acceptance. We don't get to control the unfolding of life—but we do get to choose how we respond. And that choice is where our real power lies.

Notes

INTRODUCTION

1 Richard Rohr, "Evolution of Consciousness," *Daily Meditations*, Center for Action and Contemplation, December 28, 2014. https://cac.org/daily-meditations/evolution-of-consciousness-2014-12-28/

2 Ken Wilber, *The Integral Vision: A Very Short Introduction to the Revolutionary Integral Approach to Life, God, the Universe, and Everything* (Boston: Shambhala, 2007).

THE WORK: A DAILY RHYTHM

3 Hollis, James. Living an Examined Life: Wisdom for the Second Half of the Journey. Paperback ed., Inner Traditions/Bear & Co., 2018.

THE PROBLEM: A VIRTUAL REALITY

4 James Finley, Turning to the Mystics podcast, "Thomas Merton: Session 1, Episode 4," Center for Action and Contemplation, March 2, 2020, https://cac.org/podcast/turning-to-the-mystics/

THE SOLUTION: A MOVE INWARD

5 Rick Rubin, interview with Will Smith, *Tetragrammaton*, episode aired 2023. https://tetragrammaton.com

GRIEF

6 Thomas Merton, "The Serene Disciple," in Falling Upward: A Spirituality for the Two Halves of Life by Richard Rohr (Jossey-Bass, 2011).

LARGER SELF

7 Julia Cameron, *The Artist's Way: A Spiritual Path to Higher Creativity* (New York: TarcherPerigee, 2002).

8 Judah & the Lion, "Bargaining," *The Process*, Cletus the Van Records, 2023.

www.ingramcontent.com/pod-product-compliance
Ingram Content Group UK Ltd.
Pitfield, Milton Keynes, MK11 3LW, UK
UKHW021934200726
13853UKWH00011B/1453